Where The Light Touches You

Vianne Kara Singh

BookLeaf
Publishing
India | USA | UK

where the light touches you

© 2021 Vianne Kara Singh

Presentation by *BookLeaf Publishing*

Web: www.bookleafpub.com

E-mail: info@bookleafpub.com

ISBN: 9789358360363

First edition 2021

to my brother mark, thank you for your support and encouragement in my writing throughout your life and in your absence. i hope my love transcends this lifetime and finds you where you are.

rest in eternal peace.

ACKNOWLEDGEMENT

For Tara and Siew Singh,

I am the luckiest girl in the world to be your daughter

For the army that raised me

For the women in my life who exemplify boundless love and infinite strength

For the person I'll love twice as much tomorrow

For my best friend

For the ones who constantly reassured me in this process

For the people who inspired these words and may never read them

For the ones who broke my heart

& for the ones who healed it.

Missavi, you always knew this would happen one day.

the grieving.

when you experience traumatic loss it is hard to
believe that life will give you more situations to
grieve

how can you expect me to let go when all i've
known about loss was what it took from me?

i have seen hallowed halls of hospitals

open caskets

and burning bodies

why would i actively choose to lose someone again?

i never knew peaceful endings or consensual
goodbyes

every time i have known love and loss it has been a
beautiful dance until the music cuts short

and the lights cut off

and there is an aching silence

lingering

am i wrong for trying to avoid grieving the death
of someone still breathing?

i've been trying to hang up the black dress for good

// actively learning why letting go was more about me than it was about you

you are valid in feeling through every stage of grief
in whatever order it comes to you

// calling it linear does this process injustice

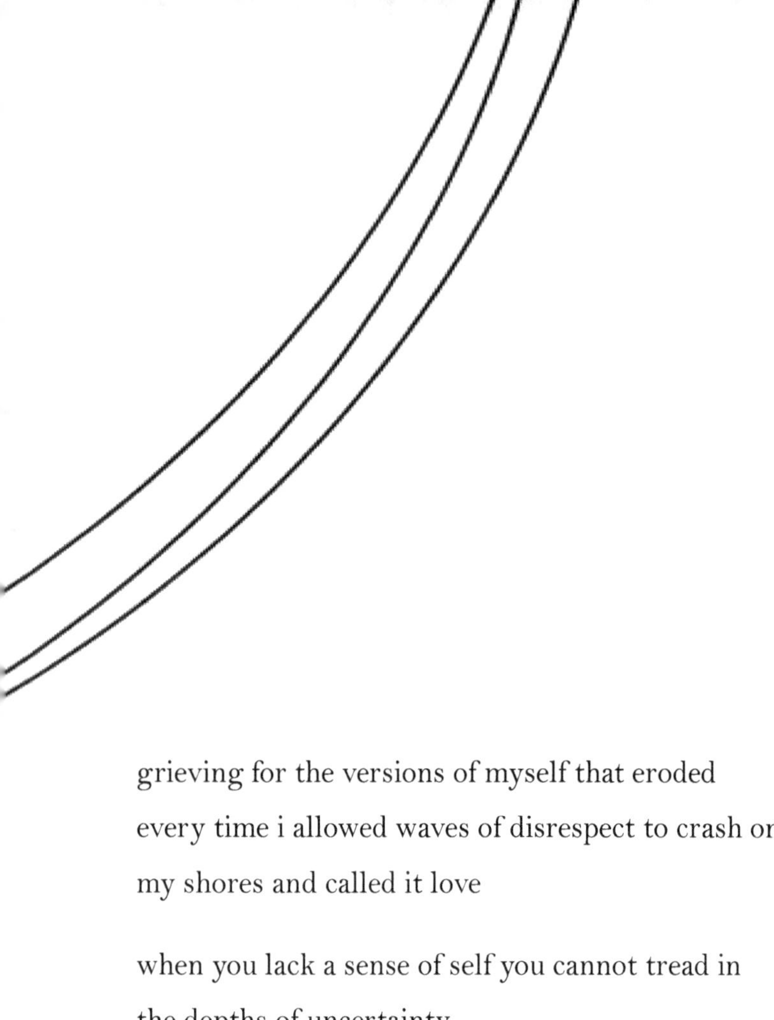

grieving for the versions of myself that eroded
every time i allowed waves of disrespect to crash on
my shores and called it love

when you lack a sense of self you cannot tread in
the depths of uncertainty

you drown.

// sink or swim the choice is ultimately yours

my trauma is like tectonic plates

the cracks that shift ever so often and ripple their
way to another part of my planet

these wounds are deceptive

i can see them so clearly where they start

the illusion of where they end

and how deep they go

the thing about trauma that nobody tells you

is that while the rest of the world continues to spin

my plates continue to shift

and nobody notices the white of my knuckles as i
hold on tight to this familiar chaos

nobody notices until it's the ground beneath them
that begins to shake

i got used to the motion sickness

i got used to the tides retreating and swelling
before they crash

i got used to the devastation i seemed to always
leave behind

there is guilt when the parts of me cross their
borders

// i'm sorry that i'm sorry about all of this

when someone leaves you abruptly

try not to mirror the grief of losses past

// you know better now, you know?

you must allow yourself permission to grieve the
things that hurt you
allow yourself the gentleness of the embraces that
may have missed you

give yourself the grace to accept
that your trauma was never your fault
and any action you take as a consequence of that
is no less valid simply because it isn't perfect

grief is a strange thing
attaching itself to you in the absence of another
on some days you can wade in its water
it feels familiar
calm

but then you feel the coldness just below you
the depth of it creeping up
and all it takes is a strange chill in the air
or a familiar scent or sound
to remind you of every moment you'll never get
back again

of every moment you'll never get to have

grief is a fickle thing
in waves some days, in specks another
i wept for years when you died
i collapsed into victimhood and for that
i felt shame

but now i know there is harm when we pity
ourselves for facing the gravity of our devastation

we must give ourselves the compassion we crave
gentle now…

// nobody told me what to do with myself after losing you

the learning/the loving.

today it feels as though i am scrubbing you from
my bones

// your stain is taking a while to fade

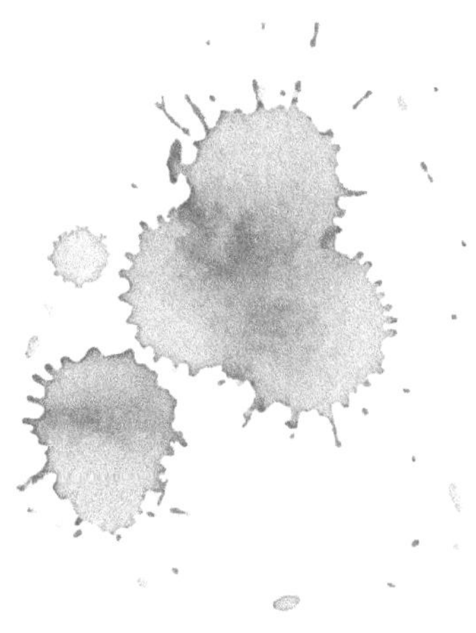

i knew we were broken long before we shattered

i am selfish in wanting one more moment

one more word

one last bit of you

as if my body does not know itself without you

you left a fingerprint on the upper right corner of
my heart

where i can feel it begging my ribs to crack open
and my brain to be quiet for one minute

you have left the kind of impression nobody will
talk about

but that i will carry with me for years

it's easy to lie about love especially in its absence

and paint the picture of strength

the brush doesn't glide smoothly any more

the paint is dried the colors have dulled

defeat is never pretty

they'll never mount our love in a museum

people will not flock in waves to gaze at this mess
and try to justify its beauty

when you catch yourself thinking of me

remember that i'll continue to leave flowers on our
unmarked grave

everyone else was tired of cleaning up the ashes we
left behind

but i still go from time to time

maybe we deserved a monument

maybe we deserved to be immortalized in the stars
the way heroes are

that's the way i choose to remember us

when i visit

that's the love i leave flowers for

// it's okay to grieve the version of love as you experienced it, it's okay to celebrate it too

you are not your father

but my god do your eyes look like his

and your hands hold women like his

and your voice commands a room like his

and if my father loved your father

the way friends who transcend lifetimes do

how could i expect to love anyone but you?

we're just keeping up tradition

// curse of our lifetimes

i can almost feel that we are bound to multiple
lifetimes

maybe in the one before we are dancing barefoot I
can almost feel your heartbeat and it matches the
song

scratchy records and warmth that doesn't go
farther than the quarter inch between our bodies In
another lifetime Our parents water our love

help us grow

your mom shares her list on how to love you

my dad wants to tell you how to be a man one day

our love sees sunlight

and the petals are soft

they extend again

into another lifetime

maybe the next

the world will have learned its lesson

and make sure to never place us too far apart

there would be no miles of ocean

no wishful thinking

no goodbyes

in another lifetime

maybe we'd get it right

and maybe we'd say everything we held in that
night

maybe we'd look back at this life and laugh

at how silly we must have been to give it all up

maybe we'd greet each other and say,

"i knew i'd find you again, it seems i always do"

// loss is a twisted lesson in value

i want to dance with you

until our feet fall off

until the records spiral out of control

i want to catch your rhythm

syncopated

unsophisticated

defying gravity through unity

i want to dance with you

i want to hear our song Feel every chord strike a
new heartbeat

my toes quietly kiss the ground to the beat that is
forever branded into my skin

i want to dance with you

i want to dance with you

as the sun settles into the moon

as the clouds roll around until there's just blurry
afternoons

that i've danced with you

i want to dance with you

i want to feel your fingers where my hip bones
stick out like the bridge of a song

your body shadowing mine

because in that moment we have intertwined

i want to dance with you

i want the whole room to stand still

i want everyone to see the electricity course
through us

around us

with us

when i dance with you

i want to dance with you

until we're old and gray

and scratchy like the records we've played

i want to dance with you

until our backs are bent

our knees are shaky

and we can't hear so well but we've memorized the
melodies

of all the songs that I've danced with you

// take my hand. take my whole life too

my skin aches at the thought

i can't wait to get my hands on you

my fingerprints leaving proof that was

here,

                     and here,

and here

// mesmerized until i can memorize you

a penny for your thoughts

have they priced second chances yet?

// spare change

i convinced myself my world would shatter without
you

i've lost so many people over the years i just
couldn't bear the thought of losing you too

when i faced death i greeted it like an old friend

numbed through the motions of the shuddering
realization that there would be a permanent gap in
my life where you once stood

i knew how to feel everything that comes with loss

a sharp unbearable pain

tears that swell but never fall

the motions of a ghost

everything and nothing all at once

i had perfected the art of losing people i loved

i perfected how to continue living after the lives i
found myself caught up in had stopped

but i also knew

that if it came down to it

and we had to say goodbye

i would never stop grieving you

i would never stop losing you

every time my eyes opened i would feel your
absence and it would cut me open and leave me to
bleed

i'd stain everything i touched

i would find you in every crowded space

i would beg for you to come back to me in loud
silence i would lay awake in darkness until it
echoed back to me in your voice

i never could let you go

and so i'll stay put

at the sacrifice of my self worth

i lay bare on the cutting block every piece of me

just to keep you for one more second

i froze near the ashes of our love

taped my eyes open praying for a spark

something to hold me over

something to keep me warm

you promised you would stay

late into the morning

when you whispered forever

that's when i bound myself to a promise

i knew in that moment that i couldn't lose someone
who's words spilled like honey out of his mouth

into my skin

but you can't tie yourself to the hollow words of
fragile men

you can't lose yourself in the ways he held your
heart

gently enough to keep it

reckless enough to make it drop from time to time
you can't make a home out of someone who lacks
the foundation to love you properly

and blame it on the lock changing

or losing the keys

or the chipped paint on the walls

as to why you never felt at home in the first place
you can't abandon yourself to keep someone

people are not our possessions

and the tighter you hold on to someone else you
will only suffocate yourself

and when you go

when this love has ended I'll burn everything to
the ground just to keep myself warm

i'll grieve you in the old familiar ways

i'll pick up the ashes and rub the soot between my
fingers

just to touch you one more time

when this love has ended

know that death and i are old friends

know that i'll put on the familiar record and dance
with the reaper himself

my head against his chest

my hand in his once more

// the finale

when lost love hollows you out

nobody will remember what you gave to save it

they'll always remind you what it took from you
though

shatter the illusion that sacrifice is the price we pay
for access to love

// love is a practice of art, not a transaction.

when he asks you to change your body for him

tell him this was made from scratch by your
mother and he can refer to her for the recipe if he
doesn't like how it tastes

when he tells you that you are a product of your
past and disregards the woman you are in that
moment

tell him looking backwards is just his way of
refusing accountability for the future

when he makes fun of the way your face is round
like the moon

tell him you wear it like the sun

the way your grandmother did

the way your daughter might too

when he twists every insecurity in you like a knife

grab a hold of it rip it out of you

point it right back at him

and even if you bleed and it drips to the floor

show him there is a warrior behind the blade

let him cower in fear that his words hold no weight
when he refuses to value you for everything that
you are

when he cannot find the magic between the details
or can't comprehend the magnitude of your moving
parts

pity him

and remind yourself that the way you see yourself
is more important

more valuable

than the ways his insecurities project themselves
on to you

*// when he disrespects you it is not your job to beg him
or teach him how to*

sometimes i think about the way you looked at her

like she was crafted just for you

how i stood in the background of your love

waiting for you to dip into me at your convenience

we weren't built from trust and i know that

i recognize that patterns and habits are just
nicknames for each other but i can't help but sink
into the darkness of comparison

this envy is a blade in my chest pocket

does my name echo in you the way hers did?

do you try to make a home out of me for the ghost
of her?

i try to come to peace with the fact that you'd never
love me the way you loved her

that she got the best of you

and i'm here picking up the pieces like always

when you say her name i can feel your heart sink
when you breathe life into the past with her i can
recognize that a part of you yearns for everything i
am not

maybe one day you'll learn to love all my moving
parts

maybe one day you'll heal and forgive her for
salting wounds of abandonment in you

maybe one day i'll learn that i'm not filling her
place but taking up my own

maybe one day i'll feel worthy of it

i wish i could learn to love you in the ways that she
did and maybe i wouldn't feel so unfamiliar and
uncomfortable to you

i wish i could be all the things you dreamed of with
her and then make room for you to dream about me

that's the cruelty of insecurity

i would peel my skin to become who you wanted

i would box in the ocean just to drown her name in the depths where you could not touch it

i would shed myself of everything i've ever known to be true

just for one minute

just to feel what it would be like to be loved by you

but self-sacrifice isn't the way to love someone

why would I want someone who puts me against someone else?

their choice has been made already hasn't it?

if you are willing to hold me to the standard of another

then you have already rejected all that I am So you learn through the cracks in your heart That you can't abandon yourself to keep someone

people are not our possessions

and the tighter you hold on to someone else

you will only suffocate yourself

i slammed every door shut

and deadbolted the frame

i changed every key

locked every window

moved far away from us

but i never could bring myself to turn the light off

the small one in the hallway

the one only you could see

the one you always forgot to turn off before you
came to bed

i always left a light on for you

maybe that way you would find your way back
home

and not feel lost as you made your way back to me
this was never that safe

the locks could be picked anyway

i had made up my mind a long time ago

we weren't going to burn like everything else

we weren't going to crumble

we weren't going to break

in the process of trying to protect us i was hurting
myself

delusions are just premonitions of heartache

// i wanted to believe what we could be

i couldn't face what we actually are

// like clockwork

the healing.

i will teach my daughter to admire the moon for
the way she dances between her shadows

the way she unapologetically rises when she is not
whole

and remains faithfully nestled among the stars

where she does not doubt for one second is where
she belongs

// a lesson in patience with processes of self

boundaries do not always have to be hostile or cold

they can be gentle

like a breeze or a sigh of relief

whispering gently, "i acknowledge your existence
as you are

while i honor my own as i am"

// you don't have to bend or break

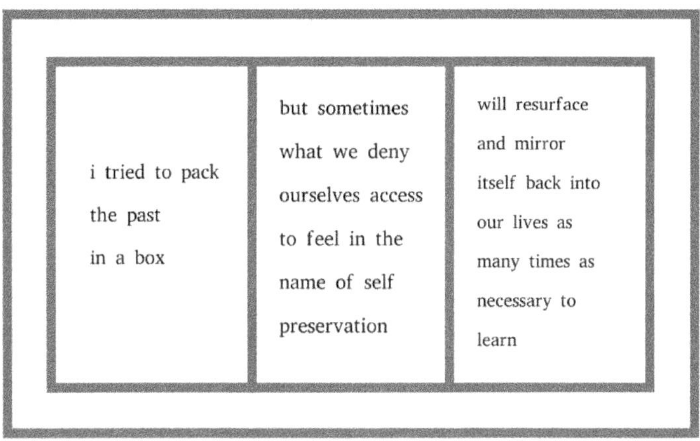

// the woman in the mirror is both a stranger and an old friend

to the women who raised me,

may we learn to love and honor your life so that your resilience isn't a reflection of your circumstances, but a virtue you share at your own discretion.

//   the things i wish i picked up from you were the things you never learned to put down

they always say, "the world is yours if you just-"

and i want to shatter the illusion that access to a
beautiful experience in this lifetime is conditional
to the way we show up for ourselves

the world is mine simply because i am made from it

i am a woman of the earth and the skies

i am generations of constellations

 i am worthy of a life in technicolor

simply because i am

// inhale, exhale

honor your pain

practice compassion

collapse if you must

rise when you are ready

understand that you will fall many times on your
journey to ascension

dust your palms

abandon preconceived notions of what your healing
should look like

we do a disservice to ourselves when we deny that

this work is sometimes lonely and painful.

sometimes i feel the wounds of the women who

came before me echoing within me

ripped from a homeland and placed on the shores of

a tiny island

cultivating the heartbeat of a nation with their bare

brown hands

the waves of the *kala pani* crashed on them for

years to come

women of indentured labor

women who made pillars out of dust

i come from a generational familiarity to pain

and submission

women whose bodies bruised from patriarchy

stomach growling and gut wrenching cries

exhausted from the residue of colonialism

but i also come from the same women

who in secret

around fires

around dirt

in consumption of remedial medicine

on the floor next to the midwife

in the blood they shed every month

or without warning

in the folklore they sang

in the *obeah* they knew

in the prayers the birthed from their wombs

those same women

despite everything

raised women

who raised me

i carry the strength of generations of women who
did not deserve their suffering

but i exist as a testament to their resilience i rise on
their supple brown shoulders

i am reaping the harvests of the seeds they sowed
many years and many lands ago and i hope that
when they see me

they laugh a big belly laugh

their smiles curve like the *caroni river*

their white scarves slide gently behind the crown
of their head

the gold bangles on the wrists glisten

and they can finally put their feet up

*// my ancestors are with me so i can recognize them
when i join them*

what if we reframed how we depend on community

it deserves to be acknowledged not just as the place
we resort to when all else has abandoned us

but as the foundation that we refuse to abandon

we crave empathy

but were force fed self-importance

when we indulge in viewing the world as a place
that owes you as an individual

we widen the debt of the collective

we must center ourselves in community

empower ourselves from within

find ourselves reflected back to us in the wounds
and the wisdoms of those around us

to exist in a world where we have forgotten that we
are a shared being

a combination of conditions

a descendent of spoken dissertations

we will isolate our capacity

we will idolize the arbitrary

revolution is poetry in motion

bodies called to action

radical ideas mobilized by the masses

we are, as a collective, everything we ever needed

it requires deep silence to hear the rumbles of
revolution that already exist within you

we must abandon the idea that what we produce in
attempt to satisfy the oppressor will never be
enough

black and brown bodies are more than just what we
can give to sustain the societies built to kill us

we must nurture dreams from the minute they are
a speck until they become stars

those who are birthed from injustice will feel their
bones ache when they see the same act being
performed somewhere else

listen to how your body responds to injustice

the world requires you to shake it

we must not fear it

we must create the space to feel the weight of the
moments we are passing through

when we allow ourselves to feel the pain of
generations of oppression we are acknowledging
that our journey to freedom is active

we raise our awareness to the reality that this work
is not over

not on a personal level

not on a communal level

we are allowing ourselves to grieve the empty
promises systems we have trusted can no longer
deliver

we must not let our trauma be commodified and
accept it as progress

every time we act in pursuit of our calling

in faith that our existence is justified

and our struggle is not the tax we pay for it

we are awakening a version of ourselves that has
been affirmed lifetimes ago

there is a version of you that understands deeply
that you are deserving of a life void of suffering

and there is no glory in pain

we will learn to heal ourselves

when we honor healing as a part of our journey to
freedom

we will also be able to honor and accept joy

*// true progress is in the moments where we are
unapologetically happy and not at the expense of another*

our soul may be muddy

and our roots may be bruised

but my god can we blossom

my god can we bloom

// daughter of immigrants, daughter of many lands

stop telling communities that are targeted disproportionately

affected

demonized

killed

harmed

threatened

discredited

and endangered by white supremacy

to express decency and forgiveness for white people who actively choose their whiteness over their humanity

the dismantling of a system that denies humanity can only happen when human emotion is unapologetically mobilized

// asé

we must not glorify the resilience of our ancestors
without acknowledging that their conditions were
a result of colonization and that trauma is
generational

it is our responsibility to decolonize and challenge
systems that are capitalist, sexist, racist, and
homophobic in nature in order to create a
sustainable future that isn't dependent on the
oppression and exploitation of our people

our humanity is not a radical idea and a new world
is possible if we demand it

in order to prepare ourselves to raise the next
generation we must unearth and heal the traumas
that were passed down to us

that requires us to have the difficult conversations
about our lived experiences

accepting these truths

and above all, taking responsibility for the way
these traumas have manifested themselves in our
own lives

healing generational trauma is not formulaic

it is the conscious choice to unlearn our
conditioning and act in faith that this work will
transform the way we raise our community moving
forward

there must be a collective ambition to heal

and a collective appreciation for joy

// we must prioritize this above all else

the way home.

as i cultivate this relationship with myself

no matter how messy

how magnificent

i am reminding myself to return

when i drift far from who i know myself to be

to appreciate the shedding of my skin and the

growth of my cells

to breathe life into the authentic versions of myself

that show up throughout this journey

to nurture myself with words filled with nectar

after all the darkness that this life will hand you

the magic lies in knowing that there is grace

and faith

and absolute beauty

if you remember to turn inward

and return to where the light touches you

// i am worthy, i am worthy, i am worthy.